PIANO
Adventures® *by Nancy and Randall Faber*
THE BASIC PIANO METHOD

CONTENTS

The interval of an **octave** spans 8 notes.

An octave is from one letter name
up or down to the *same* letter name.

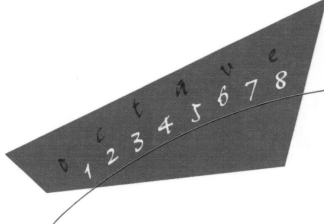

Octaves on the Staff

1. Write **octaves** on the staffs below. Then add up your points.
(Hint: Don't forget to include notes on ledger lines.)

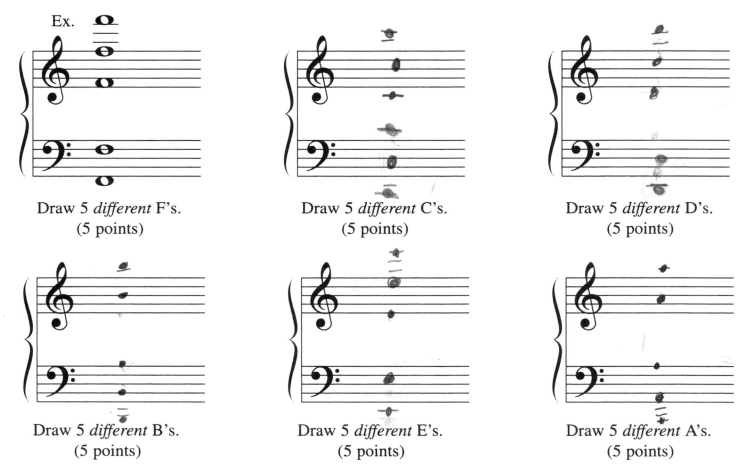

Ex.

Draw 5 *different* F's.
(5 points)

Draw 5 *different* C's.
(5 points)

Draw 5 *different* D's.
(5 points)

Draw 5 *different* B's.
(5 points)

Draw 5 *different* E's.
(5 points)

Draw 5 *different* A's.
(5 points)

2. Play each example above, moving from the *lowest* to the *highest* note. (10 pts.)

3. Circle all the **octaves** on the staff below. Hint: There are 5. (10 points)

Total Points: 50 Your Score: _____

Octave Duets

Robot Talk

4. Write **1 + 2 + 3 + 4 +** (for *1 and 2 and 3 and 4 and*) under the correct notes.
Then play this $\frac{4}{4}$ rhythm as you count aloud.

Moderato

Ex. **1   +**

(you write)

Teacher Duet: (At the lesson)

Snowflake Dance

5. Write **1 2 3 4 5 6** under the correct notes.
Then play this $\frac{6}{8}$ rhythm as you count aloud.

Andante

Teacher Duet: (At the lesson)

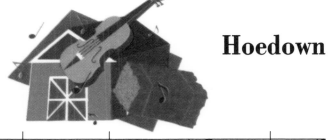

Hoedown

6. Write **1 + 2 +** under the correct notes.
Then play this **cut time** rhythm as you count aloud.

Allegro

Teacher Duet: (At the lesson)

Lessons p. 7

Ostinato

An *ostinato* is a musical pattern that is repeated over and over.

Example:

Composers from the Middle Ages to the present have used **ostinato** in music. (over 1000 years!)
Ostinato gives rhythmic motion and unity to the music.

Medieval Chant

7. a. Compose a R.H. melody for *Medieval Chant* and write it on the staff.
(Choose notes from the **D minor** 5-finger pattern.)

b. Now play your version of *Medieval Chant* and *listen* to the sound.
It may remind you of monks singing, or a shepherd's flute.

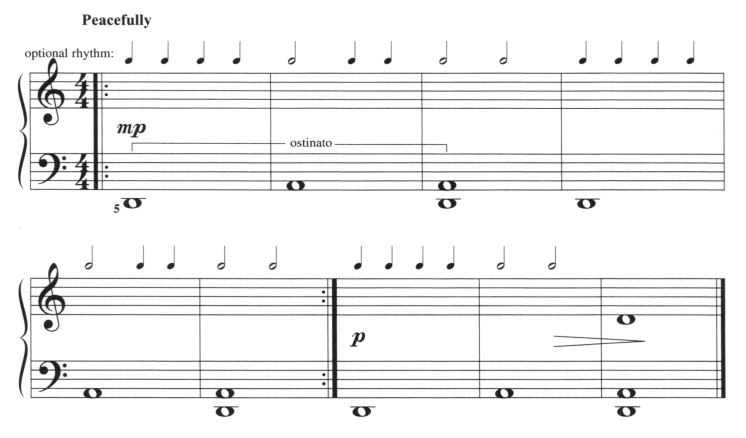

If you or your teacher have a digital keyboard, play *Medieval Chant* using the "choir" setting.
You may wish to try other settings, as well.

CLASSICAL
1750-1830

Romantic
1830-1900

Modern
1900-present

8. Can you name the **musical period** for the following pieces in your Lesson Book?

p. 7 *Minuet* by Leopold Mozart _____ *(you write)*

p. 8 *Humoresque* by Nancy Faber _____

p. 42 *Canon* by Johann Pachelbel _____

Space-Age Melody

9. a. Complete this *Space-Age Melody* by writing any L.H. whole note **octaves** below the R.H. ostinato.

b. Now play your version of *Space-Age Melody* and *listen* to the sound. (Notice the use of pedal and *sforzandos* for the L.H.)

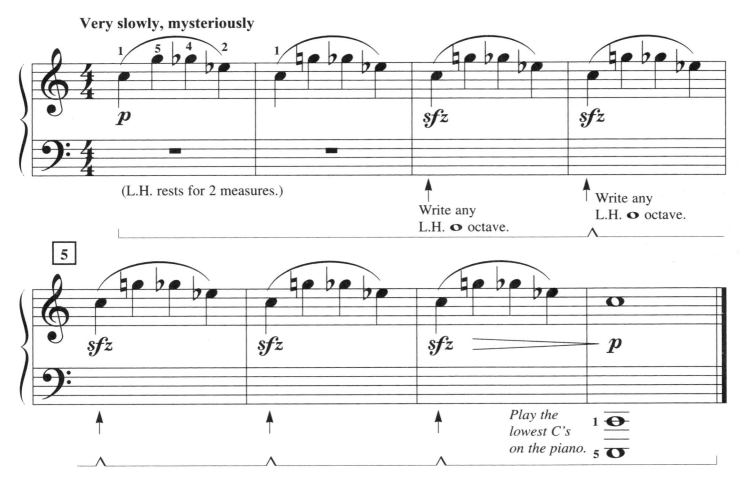

If you or your teacher have a digital keyboard, play *Space-Age Melody* using a setting you think fits the mood of the music.

Lessons p. 8

Intervals of the Major Scale

10. Play each interval formed by the shaded notes. Name the interval aloud.

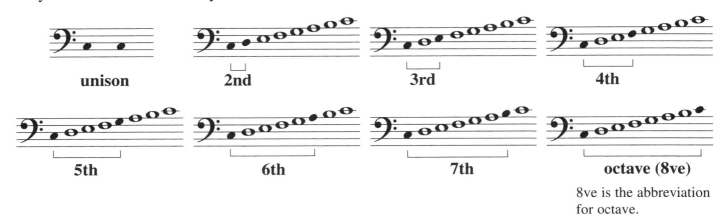

unison   2nd   3rd   4th

5th   6th   7th   octave (8ve)

8ve is the abbreviation for octave.

The Interval Trail

11.
a. Name the **key signature** for each example.
b. Complete each **major scale** by writing whole notes.
c. Name the **interval** formed by the shaded notes.

Ex: Key of _G_ major

shaded interval: _5th_

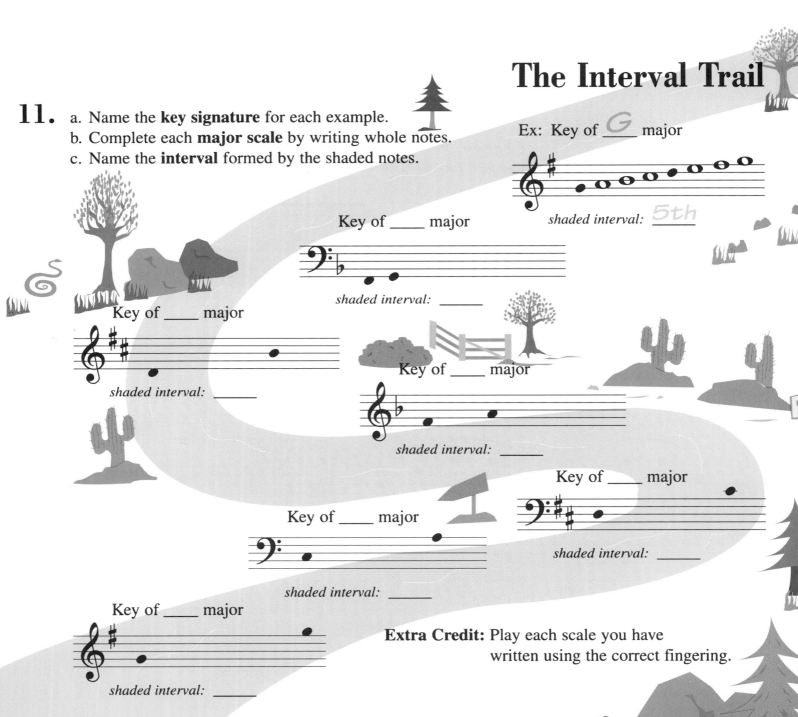

Key of _____ major

shaded interval: _____

Key of _____ major

shaded interval: _____

Key of _____ major

shaded interval: _____

Key of _____ major

shaded interval: _____

Key of _____ major

shaded interval: _____

Key of _____ major

shaded interval: _____

Extra Credit: Play each scale you have written using the correct fingering.

2.

For each example: • Find and circle every **octave**.
• Sightread the music at a moderately slow tempo.
• Then transpose to the keys suggested.

a.

Transpose to **F major** and **D major**.

b.

Transpose to **G major** and **C major**.

Now sightread hands together.

c.

Transpose to **D major** and **F major**.

3. Your teacher will play the notes of an interval separately, then together.
Listen carefully and circle either **octave** or **other interval** for what you hear.
(Hint: An octave sounds like the opening to *Somewhere Over the Rainbow.*)

1. **octave**   2. **octave**   3. **octave**   4. **octave**   5. **octave**

   or   or   or   or   or

other interval   **other interval**   **other interval**   **other interval**   **other interval**

***

For Teacher Use Only (The examples may be played in any order and repeated several times.)

Key of A Minor

Key of C major or **A minor**   **3 half steps lower**

   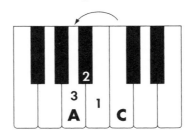

The keys of **C major** and **A minor** share the same key signature—no sharps or flats.

A minor is the RELATIVE MINOR of C major.

Count down 3 half steps from the first note of the major scale to find the relative minor key.

1. This short half-step melody will help you find the **relative minor**. MEMORIZE it, and play in lower and higher octaves.

Say or sing: "Maj-or down to min-or."   Say or sing: "Maj-or down to min-or."

Minor Tricks

(Finding the Relative Minor)

2. Play each example below. Then circle each correct example of *C down 3 half steps to A.*

FF1

A Minor Scales: Natural Minor and Harmonic Minor

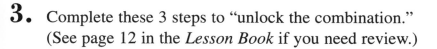

The natural minor scale—Uses only the notes of the key signature.

The harmonic minor scale—Step 7 is raised a *half step* to form the leading tone.

3. Complete these 3 steps to "unlock the combination."
(See page 12 in the *Lesson Book* if you need review.)

The Major-Minor Combination Lock

Step 1

- Write the **C major scale** using whole notes.
- Number the scale steps (1 to 8) in the blanks.
- Shade the tonic (step 1), dominant (step 5), and leading tone (step 7).

scale steps: __1__ ____ ____ ____ ____ ____ ____ ____

Step 2

- Write the **A natural minor scale** using whole notes.
- Write the L.H. fingering in the blanks.

L.H. fingering: __5__ ____ ____ ____ ____ ____ ____ ____

Step 3

- Write the **A harmonic minor scale** using whole notes.
- Shade the tonic, dominant, and leading tone.
- Circle the three half steps.

Lessons p. 12

4. **"Open the safe" by playing the following hands together:**

- Play a **C major** scale up and down hands together.
- Play an **A natural minor** scale up and down hands together.
- Play an **A harmonic minor** scale up and down hands together.

Primary Chords in A minor: i, iv, and V7

(Lower case Roman numerals indicate minor.)

In a minor key, the **i chord** and **iv chord** are minor. The **V7** is major.

5. Play each primary chord, saying its Roman numeral aloud.

G♯ is the leading tone from
the harmonic minor scale.

Musical Card Game

(Primary Chords in A minor and C Major)

6. Draw a connecting line to form "pairs of cards" with matching information.

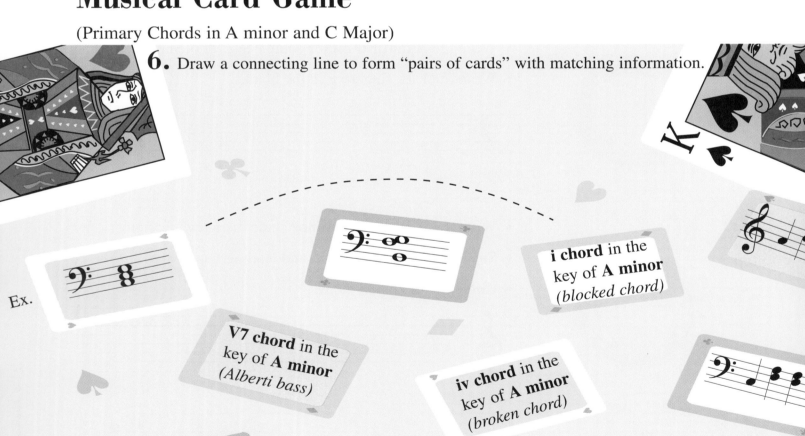

Ex.

i chord in the key of **A minor** (*blocked chord*)

V7 chord in the key of **A minor** (*Alberti bass*)

iv chord in the key of **A minor** (*broken chord*)

V7 chord in the key of **C major** (*blocked chord*)

IV chord in the key of **C major** (*waltz bass*)

Card Shark: As your teacher points to any "card," see how quickly you can play it on the keyboard!

FF

Harmonizing with i, iv, and V7 in A minor

7. Play each chord, then copy it on the staff.

i   iv   V7

(you copy)   *(you copy)*   *(you copy)*

The Wild Tarantella

8. a. First play the R.H. melody.

b. Then **harmonize** it with **i**, **iv**, or **V7 chords**. (Write two 𝄢 chords per measure.)

Hint: The notes of a chord are called *chord tones*.
Look for melody notes that match the chord tones of the **i**, **iv**, or **V7 chords**.
Listen carefully and let your ears guide you.

Lessons p. 13

Motive and Sequence

A **motive** is a short musical pattern.

A **sequence** is a musical pattern immediately repeated on another pitch. A sequence may be *higher* or *lower.*

Play:

Famous Motives and Sequences

9.
  a. Match each **motive** to its **sequence** with a connecting line.
  b. Circle whether the sequence is *higher* or *lower.*
  c. Then play the motive with its sequence on the piano.

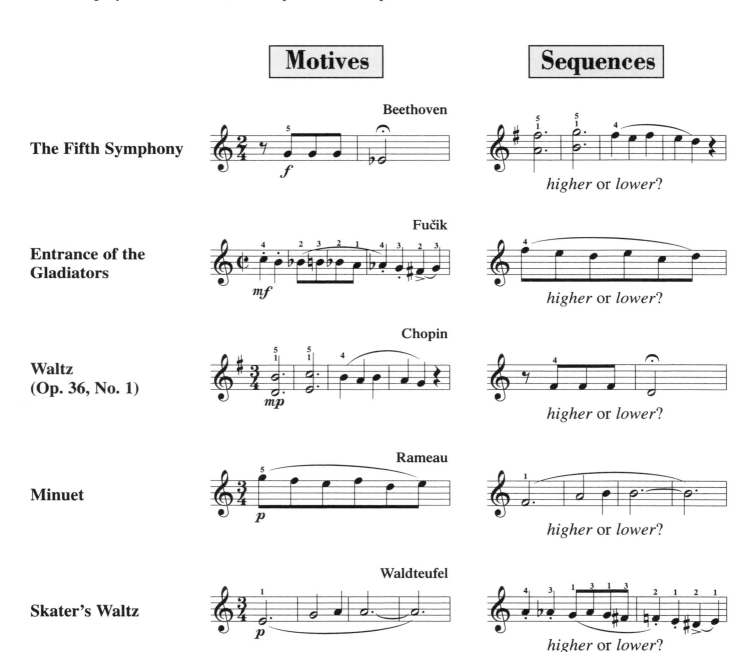

12

Primary Chords in A minor

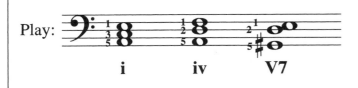

Play:

i   iv   V7

Mountain Climbing

(Sequences in A minor)

10.
a. Write **sequences** of the opening **motive** beginning on these A minor scale steps.

b. Harmonize each measure by circling **i**, **iv**, or **V7**. Then write the **blocked chord** on the staff.

c. Play and *listen*.

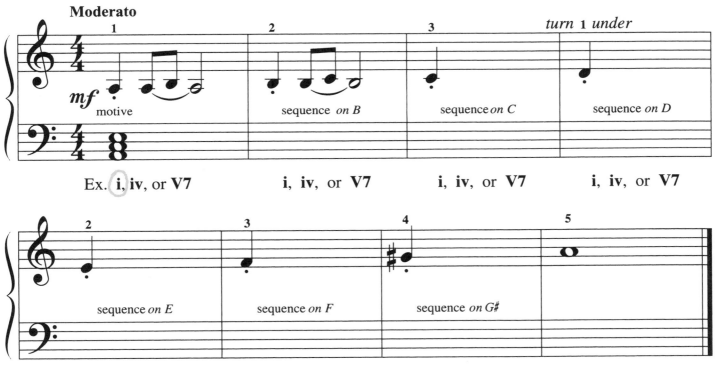

Moderato

1   2   3   *turn* 1 *under*

mf
motive   sequence *on B*   sequence *on C*   sequence *on D*

Ex. **i**, **iv**, or **V7**   **i**, **iv**, or **V7**   **i**, **iv**, or **V7**   **i**, **iv**, or **V7**

2   3   4   5

sequence *on E*   sequence *on F*   sequence *on G♯*

i, **iv**, or **V7**   **i**, **iv**, or **V7**   **i**, **iv**, or **V7**   **i**, **iv**, or **V7**

 Play *Mountain Climbing* using these 3 accompaniment patterns.

Blocked chord accompaniment   **Broken chord accompaniment**   **Alberti bass accompaniment**

legato

L.H.   L.H.   L.H.

Lessons p. 16

11.

Sightread each musical example at the tempo given.
Watch for **sequences**.
Then transpose to the keys suggested.

a.

Transpose to **D minor** and **C minor**.

b.

Transpose to **D minor** and **G minor**.

c.

Transpose to **C minor** and **G minor**.

12.

Your teacher will play a **motive** followed by a musical example which may,
or may not be a sequence. *Listen* carefully!
Circle **sequence** or **not a sequence** for what you hear.

1. **sequence**
or
not a sequence

2. **sequence**
or
not a sequence

3. **sequence**
or
not a sequence

4. **sequence**
or
not a sequence

(Your teacher may drill you with more ear training examples of **motive** and **sequence**.).

For Teacher Use Only (The examples may be played in any order and repeated several times.)
Hint: The teacher should pause briefly after the motive before completing the example.

Review (UNITS 1-2)

- Unscramble each musical term below.
  (The answers are at the bottom of the page.)

- Then **define** each term and play an example
  of each for your teacher.

Word Scrambler

(Review of Musical Terms)

Scrambled

Unscrambled

1. E V A T C O

2. O T N T S I A O

3. R A L E V I T E
   O R N I M

4. L A T A N U R
   N M O R I

5. M O N H A I C R
   I O R N M

6. T I V E M O

7. E C N E U Q E S

8. T E R V A L I N

1. octave 2. ostinato 3. relative minor 4. natural minor 5. harmonic minor 6. motive 7. sequence 8. interval

Key of D minor

Key of F major or **D minor**

3 half steps lower

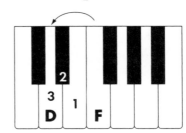

The keys of **F major** and **D minor** share the same key signature—one flat (B♭).

D minor is the RELATIVE MINOR of F major.

Review: Count down 3 half steps from the first note of the major scale to find the relative minor key.

1. This short half-step melody will help you find the **relative minor**.
MEMORIZE it, and play in lower and higher octaves.

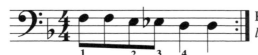 Repeat in *lower* octaves.

 Repeat in *higher* octaves.

Say or sing: **"Maj- or down to min - or."**   Say or sing: **"Maj- or down to min - or."**

More Minor Tricks

2. The tonic note of the **major key** is given.
Draw the tonic note of the **relative minor key** (3 half steps lower).

Ex.

3. The tonic note of the **minor key** is given.
Draw the tonic note of the **relative major key** (3 half steps higher).

16

FF1

D minor Scales: Natural Minor and Harmonic Minor

4. Write each **D minor scale**. (Use whole notes.) Then shade the black keys.
(See page 18 in the *Lesson Book* if you need review.)

D natural minor scale

D harmonic minor scale

The 7th tone is raised a *half step*.

Bravo Cadenzas!

5. a. Circle **D natural minor scale** or **D harmonic minor scale** for the scale used in each cadenza passage.

b. Then play each cadenza on the piano.

cadenza—a dramatic passage played freely.

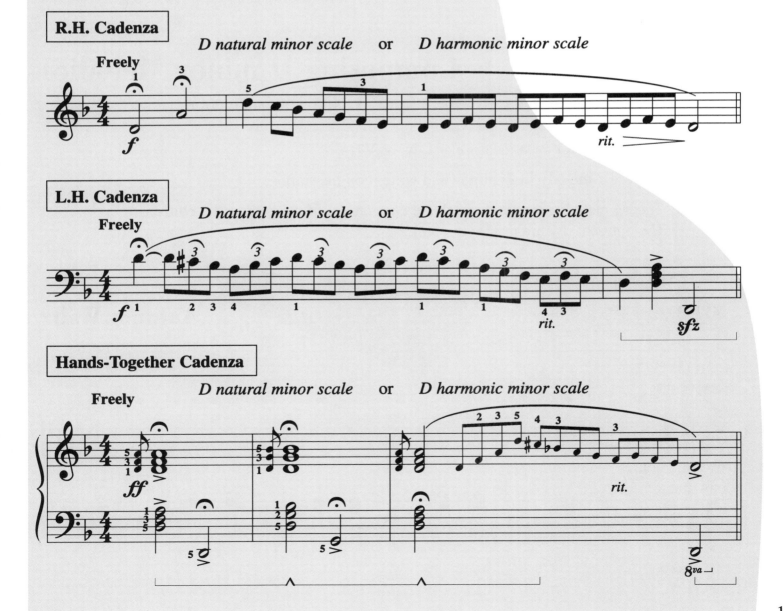

Primary Chords in D minor: i, iv, and V7

6. Play each primary chord, saying its Roman numeral aloud.

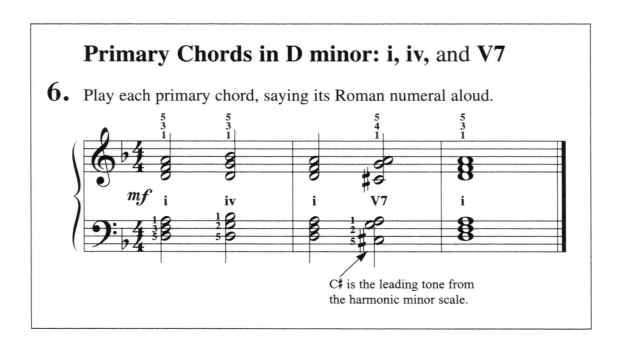

C♯ is the leading tone from the harmonic minor scale.

Composing D minor Melodies

(L.H. Accompaniment Review)

7. a. Label the harmony for each measure as **i**, **iv**, or **V7**.

    b. Then compose a **melody in D minor** and write it on the staff.

      (Hint: Choose melody notes that match the *chord tones* of the **i**, **iv**, or **V7 chords**. The optional rhythm may help you.)

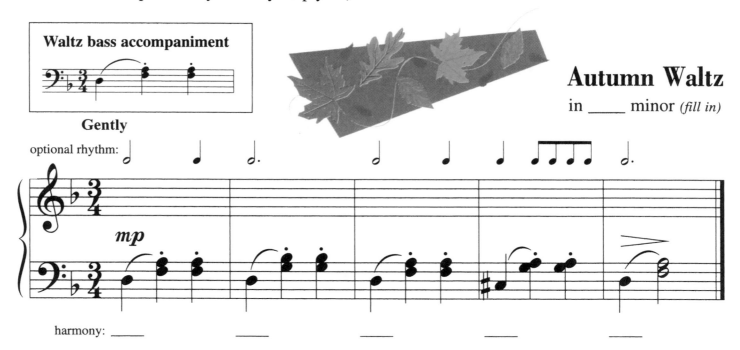

Waltz bass accompaniment

Gently

optional rhythm:

Autumn Waltz

in _____ minor *(fill in)*

harmony: _____   _____   _____   _____   _____

18

Blocked chord accompaniment

Volcanic Rock
in ____ minor

Lively
optional rhythm:

mf

harmony: ____

Broken chord accompaniment

Haunting Lullaby
in ____ minor

Slowly
harmony: ____

p

optional rhythm:

Alberti bass accompaniment

Alberti's Classical March
in ____ minor

Allegretto
optional rhythm:

mf

harmony: ____

8. Label the **motive** and circle the **sequence** in this melody.
Then sightread at a moderately slow tempo.

a.

Transpose to **A minor**.

Does this melody begin with the **natural minor** or **harmonic minor scale**? *(circle)*
Sightread at a moderate tempo.

b.

Transpose to **A minor**.

9. Your teacher will play different L.H. accompaniment patterns using
i, **iv**, and **V7 chords** in the key of D minor.

Listen carefully and circle the **last harmony you hear**.

1. **i**, **iv**, or **V7**   2. **i**, **iv**, or **V7**   3. **i**, **iv**, or **V7**

4. **i**, **iv**, or **V7**   5. **i**, **iv**, or **V7**   6. **i**, **iv**, or **V7**

(Your teacher may wish to continue this ear-training drill with more examples.)

For **Teacher Use Only** (The examples may be played in any order and repeated several times.)

A Theory Test for Your Teacher

(Key of D minor Review)

10. Help design this theory test for your teacher.
Make up a question or give some directions for each concept below.
Your instructions may ask your teacher to write chords, scales, sequences, etc. in D minor.

Be sure to check your teacher's answers and add up the points!

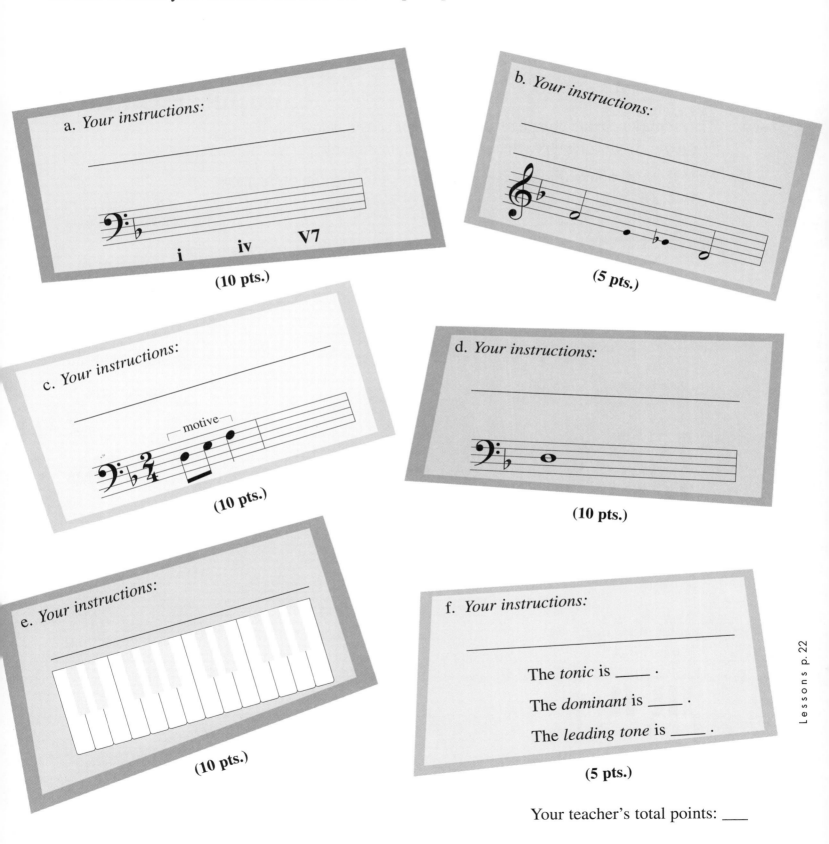

a. *Your instructions:*

_____

_____

i   iv   V7

(10 pts.)

b. *Your instructions:*

_____

_____

(5 pts.)

c. *Your instructions:*

_____

┌─ motive ─┐

(10 pts.)

d. *Your instructions:*

_____

_____

(10 pts.)

e. *Your instructions:*

_____

(10 pts.)

f. *Your instructions:*

_____

The *tonic* is _____ .

The *dominant* is _____ .

The *leading tone* is _____ .

(5 pts.)

Your teacher's total points: _____

Lessons p. 22

Major 3rd (abbreviated M3)

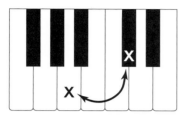

2 whole steps
(4 half steps)

melodic M3   harmonic M3

notes played   notes played
separately   together

Computer Game 1

1. a. Write a **major 3rd** to complete each computer screen below.
Be careful. Each computer screen becomes more difficult!

b. Write the total points for your correct answers at the bottom of the page.

1. Draw an **X**
UP a **M3**.

(5 pts.)

2. Draw a ○
UP a **M3**.

(5 pts.)

3. Draw an **X**
DOWN a **M3**.

(5 pts.)

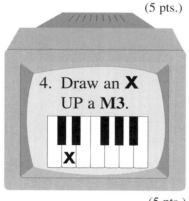

4. Draw an **X**
UP a **M3**.

(5 pts.)

5. Draw a ○
UP a **M3**.

(5 pts.)

6. Draw a ○
DOWN a **M3**.

(5 pts.)

7. Draw an **X**
UP a **M3**.

(5 pts.)

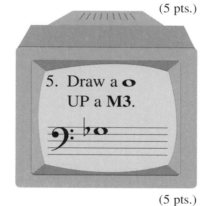

8. Draw a ○
UP a **M3**.

(5 pts.)

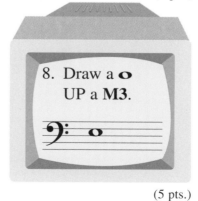

9. Draw a ○
DOWN a **M3**.

(5 pts.)

Bonus Points: Play each **M3** above on the piano.
Sing or say the letter names aloud. (5pts.)

Total points: _____

22

FF118

Minor 3rd (abbreviated m3)

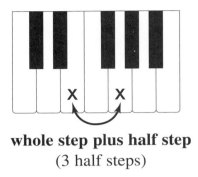

whole step plus half step
(3 half steps)

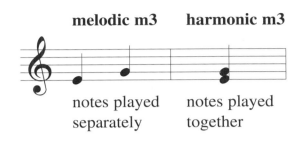

melodic m3   **harmonic m3**

notes played separately   notes played together

Computer Game 2

2.   a.   Write a **minor 3rd** to complete each computer screen below.
Think carefully. Each computer screen becomes more difficult!

    b.   Write the total points for your correct answers at the bottom of the page.

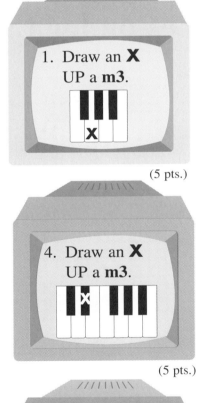

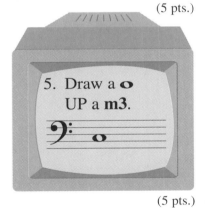

Bonus Points: Play each **m3** above on the piano.
Sing or say the letter names aloud. (5pts.)

Total points: _____

F1181

23

Major and Minor Triads

A **triad** is a 3-note chord built in **3rds**.

The 3 notes of a triad are the **root**, **3rd**, and **5th**.

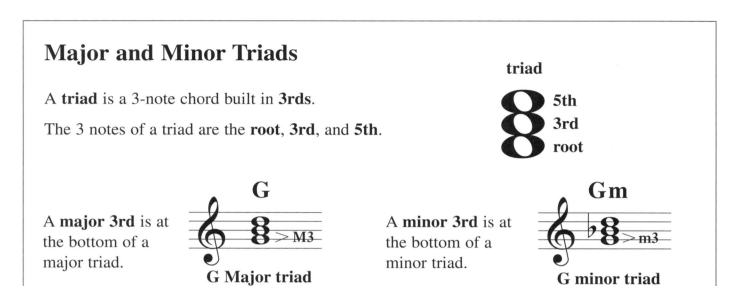

A **major 3rd** is at the bottom of a major triad.

A **minor 3rd** is at the bottom of a minor triad.

Music Lesson for Cats

3. a. These cats are meowing to **major** and **minor triads**.
Write the correct **chord letter name** above the staff for each triad.

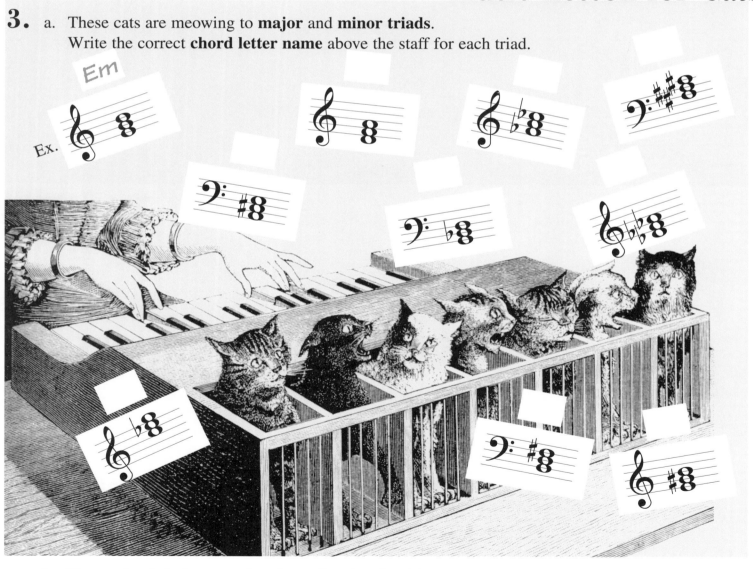

b. Play each triad above on the piano. Say the chord letter name aloud.

FF1

Review: The notes of a triad are called **chord tones**.

The Lost Chord Tones

4. a. Name the **chord tone** (root, 3rd, or 5th) that is missing from each triad.
   b. Then draw the *missing note* on the staff. (Remember the sharp or flat, if needed.)

C

Ex. missing *3rd*

Fm

missing ____

Db
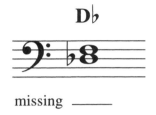
missing ____

D
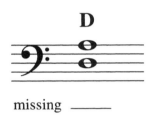
missing ____

Am
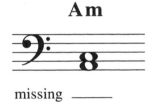
missing ____

E
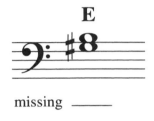
missing ____

Gm
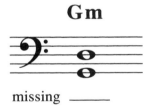
missing ____

F#
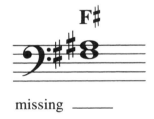
missing ____

Bb
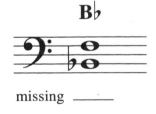
missing ____

Cm
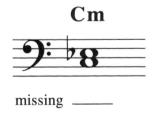
missing ____

Em
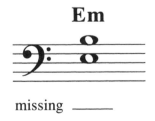
missing ____

Ab
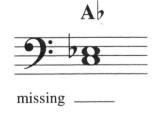
missing ____

Lessons p. 26

5. Your teacher will choose several of the triads above.
   Play each selected triad with these **4 accompaniment patterns**.

blocked chord   broken chord   waltz chord   Alberti bass pattern

Examples:

Bowling for Triads

6.   a.   First name the **scale** that is shown by the bowling pins.

       b.   Then name **two triads** that can be formed from the bowling pins that are **standing**.
           (Each pin may be used only once.)

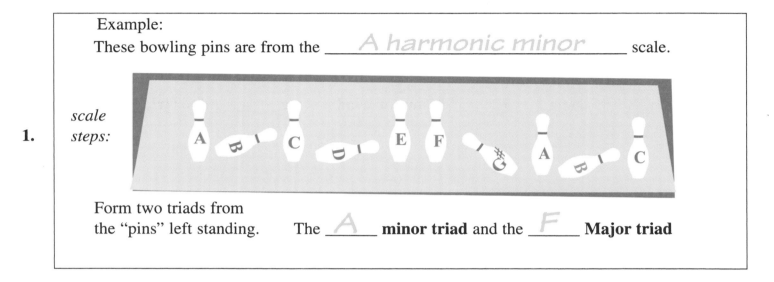

Example:
These bowling pins are from the _____A harmonic minor_____ scale.

1.   *scale steps:*

Form two triads from
the "pins" left standing.   The __A__ **minor triad** and the __F__ **Major triad**

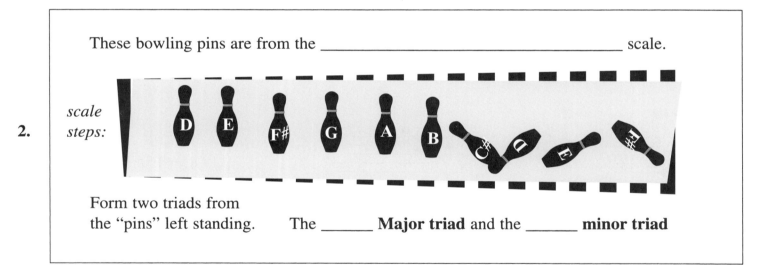

These bowling pins are from the _____ scale.

2.   *scale steps:*

Form two triads from
the "pins" left standing.   The _____ **Major triad** and the _____ **minor triad**

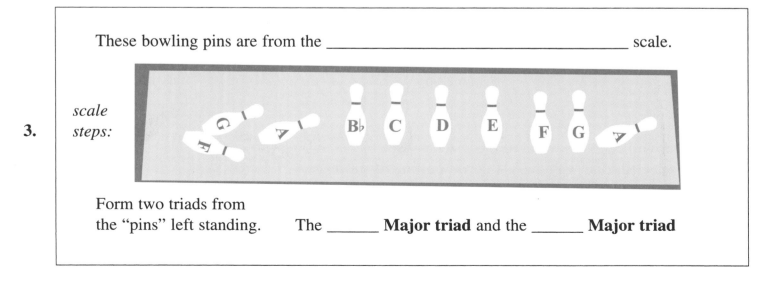

These bowling pins are from the _____ scale.

3.   *scale steps:*

Form two triads from
the "pins" left standing.   The _____ **Major triad** and the _____ **Major triad**

4.

These bowling pins are from the _____ scale.

scale steps:

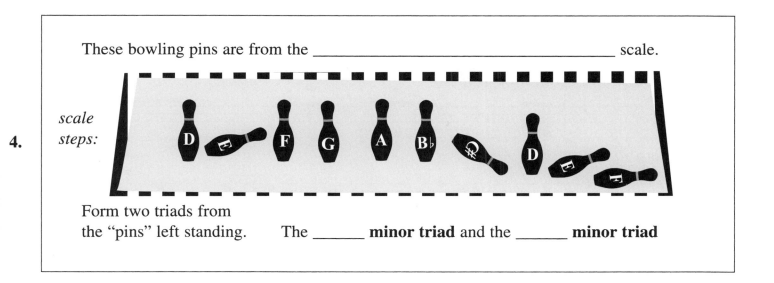

Form two triads from the "pins" left standing. The _____ **minor triad** and the _____ **minor triad**

5.

These bowling pins are from the _____ scale.

scale steps:

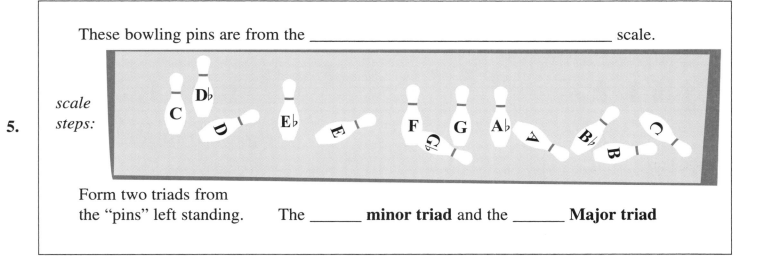

Form two triads from the "pins" left standing. The _____ **minor triad** and the _____ **Major triad**

6.

These bowling pins are from the _____ scale.

scale steps:

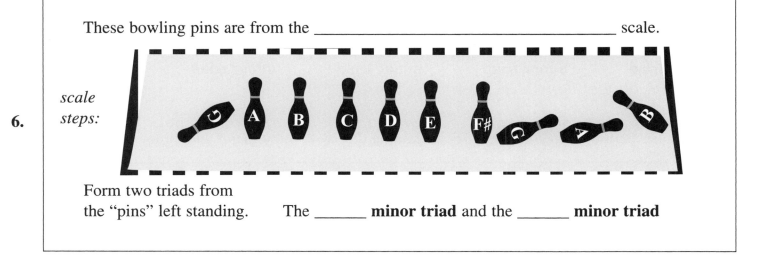

Form two triads from the "pins" left standing. The _____ **minor triad** and the _____ **minor triad**

7. Sightread this musical example. Watch for **major** and **minor broken triads**.

Hint: Count one "free" measure (*"1 2 3 4 5 6"*) before beginning.

a.

optional

Transpose to **A major** and **E major**.

Sightread this musical example. Watch for **syncopation**!
Hint: Name the **root of each triad** before playing.

b.

Transpose to **D major** and **G major**.

8. Your teacher will play an accompaniment pattern that uses a
major triad or **minor triad**.

Listen carefully! Then circle **major triad** or **minor triad** for the sound you hear.

1. **major triad**   2. **major triad**   3. **major triad**   4. **major triad**   5. **major triad**

   or   or   or   or   or

minor triad   **minor triad**   **minor triad**   **minor triad**   **minor triad**

(Your teacher may wish to continue this ear-training drill with more major and minor triads.)

For Teacher Use Only (The examples may be played in any order and repeated several times.)

FF1

First Inversion Triads

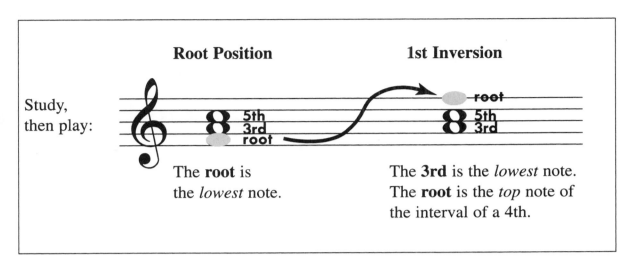

Study,
then play:

Root Position

5th
3rd
root

The **root** is
the *lowest* note.

1st Inversion

root
5th
3rd

The **3rd** is the *lowest* note.
The **root** is the *top* note of
the interval of a 4th.

Topsy-Turvy Triads

1. Do the following for each example.

a. Shade the **root**, then name the root position triad.
b. Draw the **1st inversion triad**.
c. Label the interval of a **4th** with a wedge (>). Then shade the **root**.

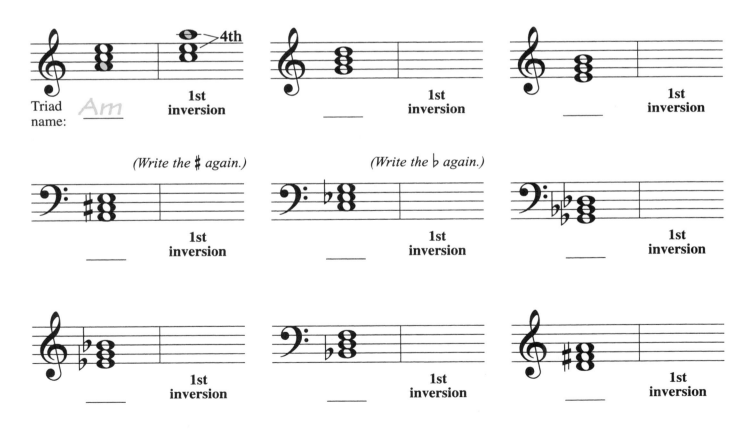

Now play these **root position** and **1st inversion triads**.
Hint: For R.H. 1st inversion chords, use fingers 1-2-5. (For L.H., use 5-3-1)

F1181

Lessons p. 30

Review:

The UPPER NOTES of a 1st inversion triad form the interval of a **4th**.

The **root** is the **top note of the 4th**.

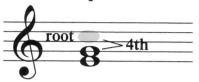

Doorbell Chimes

Each doorbell is chiming the notes of a **root position** or **1st inversion triad**.

2. a. Find and circle the **root**.

b. Then write **root pos.** (for root position) or **1st inv.** (for 1st inversion) in the blank.

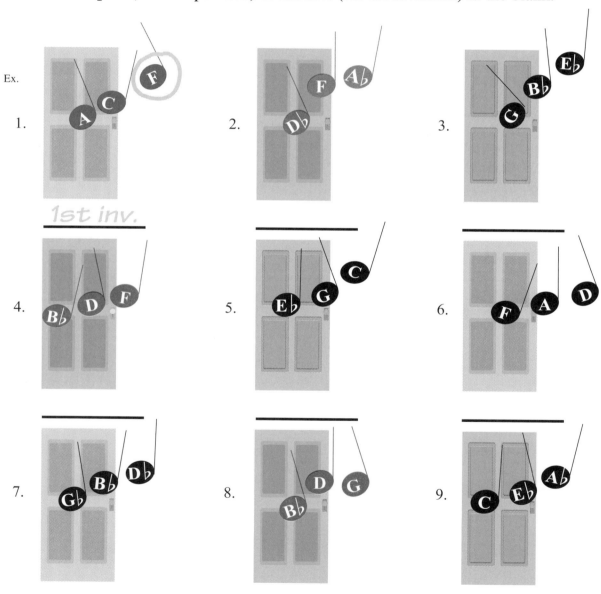

Ex.

1. A C (F)   *1st inv.*

2. Db F Ab

3. G Bb Eb

4. Bb D F

5. Eb G C

6. F A D

7. Gb Bb Db

8. Bb D G

9. C Eb Ab

SUPER STUDENT! Play each "doorbell chime" on the piano with your R.H., then L.H.
(Hint: Be sure to use the correct fingering.)
Is each triad **major** or **minor**?

3.
First name each key.
Then scan the music for **root position** and **1st inversion triads**.
Sightread each musical example at a moderately slow tempo.

Key of _____ Major / minor (*circle*)

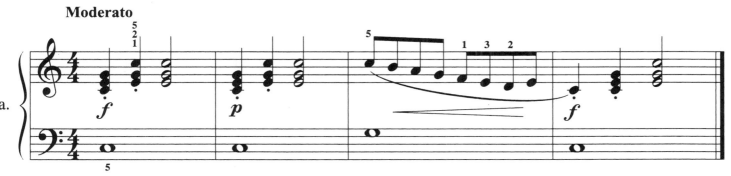

Transpose to **G major**.

Key of _____ Major / minor (*circle*)

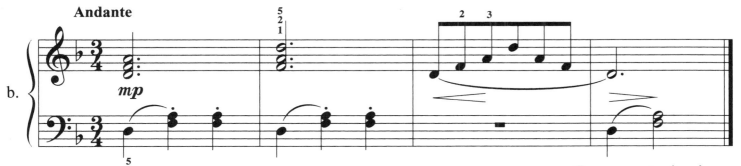

Transpose to **A minor**.

4.
Your teacher will play **example a** or **example b**.

Listen carefully! Then circle the example you heard.

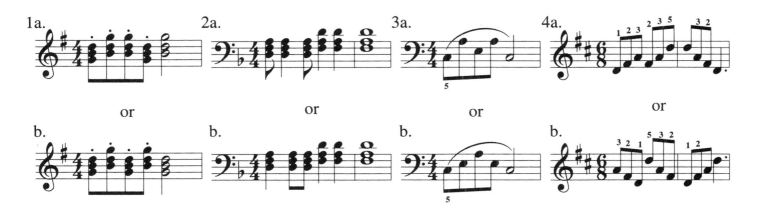

Lessons p. 32

Extra Credit: Sightread each ear-training example for your teacher.

Root Position	1st Inversion	2nd Inversion

Study, then play:

Root Position — 5th / 3rd / root
The **root** is the lowest note.

1st Inversion — root / 5th / 3rd
The **3rd** is the lowest note. The root is the *upper note* of the 4th.

2nd Inversion — 3rd / root / 5th
The **5th** is the lowest note. The root is the *upper note* of the 4th.

Triad Flips

5. Complete each example below. (The first one has been done for you.)

Ex. a.

Mark the 4th and shade the **root**.
(circle) Root pos. / **1st inv.** / 2nd inv.

Mark the 4th and shade the **root**.
Root pos. / 1st inv. / **2nd inv.**

Shade the **root**.
Root pos. / 1st inv. / 2nd inv.

b.

Shade the **root**.
(circle) Root pos. / 1st inv. / 2nd inv.

Mark the 4th and shade the **root**.
Root pos. / 1st inv. / 2nd inv.

Mark the 4th and shade the **root**.
Root pos. / 1st inv. / 2nd inv.

c.

Mark the 4th and shade the **root**.
(circle) Root pos. / 1st inv. / 2nd inv.

Shade the **root**.
Root pos. / 1st inv. / 2nd inv.

Mark the 4th and shade the **root**.
Root pos. / 1st inv. / 2nd inv.

d.

Mark the 4th and shade the **root**.
(circle) Root pos. / 1st inv. / 2nd inv.

Mark the 4th and shade the **root**.
Root pos. / 1st inv. / 2nd inv.

Shade the **root**.
Root pos. / 1st inv. / 2nd inv.

Extra Credit: Play each chord on the piano, naming its position aloud.

FF1

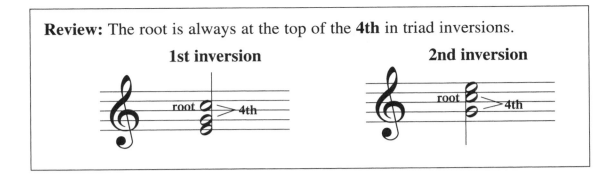

1st inversion   2nd inversion

Basketball Hoops

6. Complete each **triad inversion** at the bottom of the page by drawing a line from the correct basketball into the hoop. (You may look at the keyboard, if you wish.)

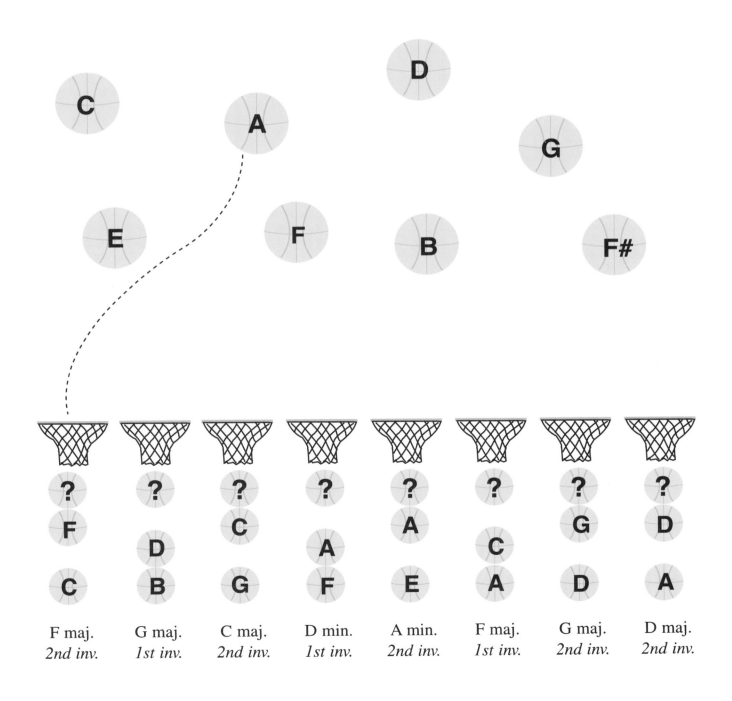

| F maj. | G maj. | C maj. | D min. | A min. | F maj. | G maj. | D maj. |
| *2nd inv.* | *1st inv.* | *2nd inv.* | *1st inv.* | *2nd inv.* | *1st inv.* | *2nd inv.* | *2nd inv.* |

7. How fast can you **play** and **name aloud** root position, 1st inversion, and 2nd inversion triads?

Your teacher will "time" you over several lessons.

1st timing: _____ *seconds*   **2nd timing:** _____ *seconds*   **3rd timing:** _____ *seconds*

a.    b.    c.

d.    e.    f.

g.    h.    i

8. Your teacher will play a triad inversion using one of these **accompaniment patterns**:

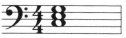         

blocked chord   **broken chord**   **waltz bass**   **Alberti bass**

Listen carefully! Then write the name of the accompaniment pattern you heard in the blank.

1. _____   3. _____

2. _____   4. _____

(Your teacher may continue this ear-training drill with more major and minor triads.)

For Teacher Use Only (The examples may be played in any order and repeated several times.)

mf   *mp*   *mf*   *mp*

FF1

Review (UNITS 1-5)

Write the correct answer in the blank for each "day of music."

The 12 Days of Music

1. On the first day of music
   my teacher gave to me,

   an _____
   (interval name)

   in a pear tree.

2. On the second day of music
   my teacher gave to me,

   two _____
   (*major* or *minor 3rds*?)

3. On the third day of music
   my teacher gave to me,

   three _____
   (*half* or *whole steps*?)

4. On the fourth day of music
   my teacher gave to me,

   four _____
   (*major* or *minor scales*?)

5. On the fifth day of music
   my teacher gave to me,

   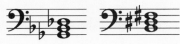
   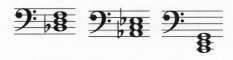

   five _____
   (*major* or *minor chords*?)

6. On the 6th day of music
   my teacher gave to me,

   six music _____(s)
   (*short musical patterns*)

(see page 12)

7. On the 7th day of music …*etc.*

   seven _____(s)
   (*patterns repeated on
   another pitch*)

8. On the 8th day … *etc.*

   eight _____ basses
   (*accompaniment pattern*)

9. On the 9th day … *etc.*

   nine _____
   (*1st or 2nd inversions*)

10. On the 10th day … *etc.*

    Play 10 times!

    ten _____(s)
    (*notes accented
    between the beats*)

11. On the 11th day … *etc.*

    eleven _____ notes
    (*the smaller notes*)

12. On the 12th day … *etc.*

    Play 12 times!

    twelve _____ scales
    (*name this scale*)

Lessons p. 36

181

35

16th Notes

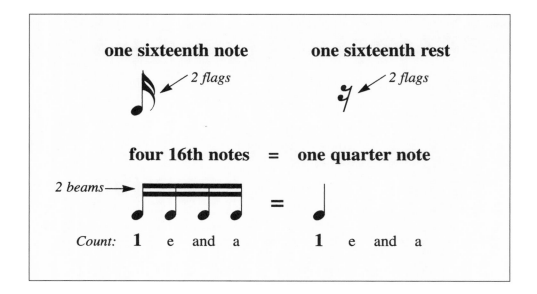

one sixteenth note — 2 flags

one sixteenth rest — 2 flags

four 16th notes = one quarter note

2 beams →

Count: **1** e and a   **1** e and a

Rhythm Words

1. Tap each **16th note pattern**. Then *listen* as your teacher taps one of the 3 rhythms.
Which rhythm did you hear? (Do this listening drill several times.)

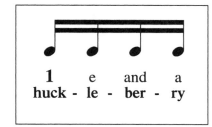

1 e and a
huck - le - ber - ry

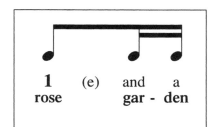

1 (e) and a
rose **gar - den**

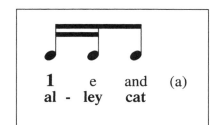

1 e and (a)
al - ley **cat**

2. Say aloud each word (or words) below, *listening* to the rhythm.
Then write the **16th note rhythm** from above that matches the sound.

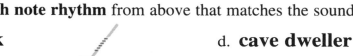

a. **hockey stick**

rhythm: [ ]

(you write)

b. **train station**

rhythm: [ ]

c. **hot potato**

rhythm: [ ]

d. **cave dweller**

rhythm: [ ]

e. **parachute**

rhythm: [ ]

f. **January**

rhythm: [ ]

The Rhythm Pyramid

3. Complete this Rhythm Pyramid by writing ♩, ♩, ♪♪, or ♬♬ notes.

a. Write **2 notes** that equal a whole note.

These notes are called

_____
(fill in)

b. Write **4 notes** that equal a whole note.

These notes are called

_____
(fill in)

c. Write **8 notes** that equal a whole note.
(Hint: Beam the notes in groups of 4.)

These notes are called

_____
(fill in)

d. Write **16 notes** that equal a whole note.
(Hint: Beam the notes in groups of 4.)

These notes are called

_____
(fill in)

4. Choose any key on the piano and set a **moderately slow steady beat**.
(Suggestion: Set the metronome at ♩ = **80**.)

Then play the Rhythm Pyramid from the *top to the bottom*.
(Hint: Play the 16th notes lightly to help your wrist stay relaxed.)

5. **Repeat Step 4**, now playing the Rhythm Pyramid from the *bottom to the top*.
Feel a steady beat throughout!

6. With the metronome set at ♩ = **80**, your teacher will point to any level
of the Rhythm Pyramid. Begin playing at that level as your teacher points.

Mystery Rhythms

7. a. Write **1 e and a   2 e and a**, *etc.* under each beat of rhythm.
Note: Write a plus for the "and": **1 e + a**

b. Tap the rhythm, counting aloud.

c. Then match each rhythm to the appropriate song title with a connecting line.
(Your teacher may sing the opening measures of each song for you.)

Yankee Doodle

*Yankee Doodle went to town,
riding on a pony.*

Jingle Bells

*Jingle bells, jingle bells,
jingle all the way.*

Twinkle, Twinkle Little Star

*Twinkle, twinkle, little star,
How I wonder what you are.*

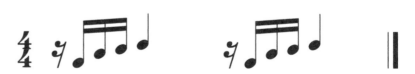

When the Saints Go Marching In

*Oh, when the saints,
go marching in,*

8.  Circle this rhythm each time it occurs: ♩♪♪♪♩
Then tap the rhythm as you count aloud, **"1 e and a,"** *etc.*
Sightread at a moderate tempo.

Key of _____ Major / minor *(circle)*

a.

Transpose to **A major** and **E major**.

Circle this rhythm each time it occurs: ♪♩♩
Then tap the rhythm as you count aloud, **"1 e and a,"** *etc.*
Sightread at a moderate tempo.

Key of _____ Major / minor *(circle)*

b.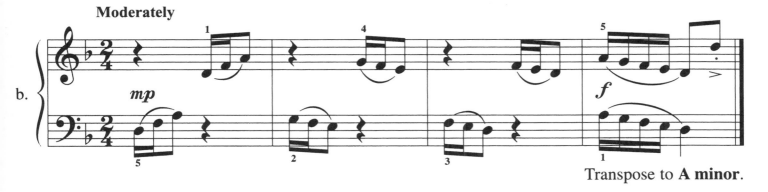

Transpose to **A minor**.

9. Your teacher will choose a key on the piano and play either **example a** or **example b**.

Listen carefully and circle the rhythm you hear.

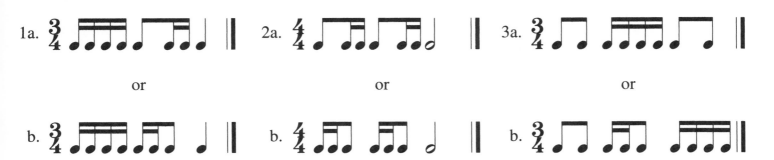

Extra Credit: Do this ear-training drill with your teacher as the student.
You tap either **example a** or **example b** on the closed keyboard cover.
Did your teacher select the correct rhythm? Have fun!

Lessons p. 42

Final Review (UNITS 1-5)

House of Riddles

Complete each riddle by writing a **musical word** that you have learned in *Level 3B*.

1. What interval begins and ends with the same note name?

   answer: _____

2. What tiny note is played quickly into the note that follows it?

   answer: _____

3. Which minor scale has **G♯** as the *leading tone*?

   answer: _____

4. What 2 intervals did Beethoven use to begin his famous 5th Symphony?

   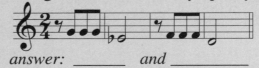

   answer: _____ and _____

5. Which triad position uses the same letter names as the root position, but has the **interval of a 4th at the top**?

   answer: a _____ triad

6. What note carries 2 flags?

   answer: _____

7. Which form of the **minor scale** uses exactly the same notes as its relative major scale?

   answer: _____

8. What kind of rhythm sounds STRONG but accents the *weak* part of the beat?

   answer: _____

The House of Riddles

9. Which **primary chord** is **major** in both a major and minor key?

   answer: _____

10. What is the name of the pianist who has completed *Level 3B Theory* and is ready to begin *Theory Level 4*?

    answer: _____

Congratulations!

(Turn the page upside down to check your answers.)

FF1